The Ultimate Guide to Safe Travel for Women

Safe Travel Tips for the Modern Woman

K. PAIGE ENGLE

Copyright © 2015 K. Paige Engle

Published by Engle Publishing
Milwaukee, WI

Copy Editor Gale E.
Cover Photography by K. Paige E.
Cover design by Beth O.

Printed in the United States of America

ISBN: 069252357X
ISBN-13: 978-0692523575

DEDICATION

To Peter and Robert

To husband, Peter and son, Robert
without whose love, patience and support,
this book would still be just a dream.

We have and will continue
to travel the world together
always.

CONTENTS

Acknowledgments

Introduction

ACKNOWLEDGMENTS

I would like to express my sincerest gratitude to my parents, Violet and Romeo for their vision of what my life would be and for sacrificing to make sure it came to be.

I would like to thank my husband, Peter for his unwavering support of all my endeavors and his continual ability to make me laugh in any situation.

To my son, Robert for giving me a reason to live my best life.

To my editor, Gale for her attention to detail and hours of assistance in making this book possible. God has truly blessed us to have you in our lives.

To countless family and friends who have been along with me through the years on my travel journeys and all those who live by my motto: Have Passport! Safe Travel!

Merci Beaucoup!

Introduction

Have you ever had to travel for business? Did you travel alone?

Have you ever been in a travel situation that you just didn't quite know how to handle?

In today's world, more women are traveling, either alone or with family than ever. According to a survey by Yahoo, 72% of women traveled solo last year. Do you know what to do in the case of an emergency? What would you do if you are mugged? What if you need medical attention? What if your passport is stolen? Who do you turn to? Whether you want to admit it or not, having travel knowledge is essential for women.

In this travel guide I am going to share tips and tricks to help you travel with ease whatever your destination. I wish I had this book when I began traveling more than 20 years ago. This guide is not only for the beginner but also for the seasoned female traveler who wants to have some extra tricks to pull out of her stylish carry-on.

As a woman who has traveled to 20 countries and 300 cities worldwide, many of them solo, I have learned strategies about traveling you need to know. Policies and attitudes differ from country to country. Consider me your personal guide.

I have traveled for business and pleasure and find different joys in each one. I have always been the one traveling alone. Traveling alone brings out an entirely different dynamic, but with a little guidance you can overcome any challenges. Whether you are single, married, or traveling with your family, this book is full of tips and tricks and will be your go-to travel guide in the future.

Regina, an executive new to international travel says, "I wish I had this advice in my 20s. It would have reduced my fear and I could have seen a lot more of the world. I would have embraced the previous travel opportunities presented to me and not denied them." Regina now travels 35% of her time and has been promoted 3 times since seeking my advice.

You will use this guide over and over again to get the answers to your safe travel questions and I guarantee that you will tell your friends. This guide is the manual that you have been looking for. It provides quick advice, relevant stories and practical tips that you can use immediately after buying your airline ticket.

Don't be the passenger with five suitcases or lost in translation. Up your travel game and impress all of your friends with this travel knowledge.

If you want practical tips and travel information that will keep you safe and savvy, read this guide. And if you have anyone in your life that is traveling in the near future, give them this guide. For more tips, etiquette and travel tales please visit: http://www.parisbypaige.com/books and sign up for my travel newsletter.

Travel can bring out the best in people and is filled with hilarious situations as if they were right off your reality TV screen. In *The Ultimate Guide to Safe Travel for Women*, I am going to be discussing the good, bad, and ugly of travel. With a little guidance you will travel with confidence and ease every time.

CHAPTER ONE

Destination Research

Imagine arriving in Hong Kong, China at 8:30 p.m. local time. You have just traveled 20 hours from the US with a layover in Tokyo, Japan. You are exhausted, hungry and want to find a pillow to lay your head. You finally make it through customs and secure your luggage when you're hit by the sweltering steam of the city. You look around for a taxi and get into the first one that arrives. Once inside the car, the driver demands money for the toll and practically snatches your wallet out of your hand. With the airport behind you, he turns into a dark alley and stops the car. He is yelling at you in Cantonese and you have no clue what he is saying. Something is seriously wrong with this picture. Suddenly a second man emerges from the shadows and they begin to talk frantically. This is NOT right. The men are screaming at each other and looking at you. It is now time to run for your life. You run down the alley with the men yelling, chasing after you. You run into a busy intersection. They stop their pursuit and you start screaming for help. Another taxi, this time an authorized one, pulls up with a family inside. They try to help you with their broken English. They whisk you inside the taxi and take you to the nearest American brand hotel so someone can translate for you. The hotel staff alerts the authorities and gets you to your hotel safely. You have just had your first encounter with an attempted kidnapping by not having arranged transportation waiting for you in a new city or destination.

Guide books/tourist bureaus

There are a multitude of guide books, travel apps and tourist bureaus available to help you with your research prior to travel. I advise people to ask for recommendations from family and friends. Practically every city has a tourism or visitor's board to help you discover and enjoy the destination. Contacting them and visiting their websites can provide a wealth of knowledge and current events. There may be deals and tourist cards provided by tourist boards and visitors' bureaus to give you an unforgettable overview of the city. It is also advisable to research the crime and security situations of each destination that you plan to visit. This information is critical to safe travel.

Language Knowledge

Having some language knowledge can make or break your travel experience. I advise learning the language or at least a few key phrases. It will be helpful in navigating a new destination. Local language classes and/or tutors can help you grasp the language. There are several computer, apps, home programs, and/or tutors via Skype available. The immersion method is the best if you need to learn it quickly and offers the most absorption of the language nuances and colloquial vocabulary. It is geared toward living the language in everyday situations. I am lucky enough to have a working knowledge of 5 languages and speak 2 fluently, without that I am not sure that I would have had the confidence to travel alone all of these years. It was extremely helpful in navigating the cities and countries while traveling. I would never diminish the tremendous benefits of knowing a foreign language.

I am one of the most vocal foreign language evangelists you will ever meet. Many people have survived without it, but knowing a little of the language makes your adventure much more memorable and fun.

Personal recommendations

Ask your family, friends, colleagues, and contacts to discover who has been to the destination. Don't forget to ask them about their favorite hotels, restaurants and activities. These are some of the best opinions that you can get.

Use the internet

The internet is an invaluable resource for you. If you do not have the time, have your assistant/intern research your destination. It will be a great exercise in data mining and reporting for them. Don't forget your corporate travel department. These professionals deal with travel daily and are full of information and resources.

Passports & Visas

Each US citizen must have a valid passport to travel internationally. It is important that your passport be valid during all the periods that you plan to travel. Most countries in the Schengen Region (Western Europe) require a passport to be valid for at least 6 months from the first date of entry, otherwise it will be denied. Consult your embassy website for Visa entry requirements. There may also be limitations on the length of stay.
Keep your passport protected at all times during international travel, either in a money belt or in a hotel front desk safe. You do not want to fall victim to pickpockets or thieves that prey on tourists in many destinations around the world.

After a day of sightseeing, one of my clients, Lori L., decided to use her free time in the city and go shopping. She had been warned about the pickpocket situation in Europe, but she thought that since she was from a major city in the USA, she really did not need to worry. She was wrong. Her passport, credit card and money were stolen while she waited to cross the street at a stop light. The thief bumped her lightly at the curb as it filled with people waiting to cross. The light changed, everyone crossed and before she realized what had happened, her passport and money were gone.

She came back frantically to our hotel and alerted me of the horrible situation. This was the first time in my 25 years of traveling and leading groups that I have had such an event happen. I jumped into action and was able to get her a new passport the next day within 4 hours. That is the beauty of having a knowledgeable guide who knows the language and culture and who is effective when it matters the most.

6

Transportation [metro/bus/train/bike/car/taxi]

Prepare for your mode of transportation. Some people overlook this and then try to wing it. Think safety first.

Late airport arrivals and delays can put you in a bind and you will be caught off guard if you do not prepare ahead of time. Line up at an official taxi stand and make sure to have your destination written on a card in the local language. I would also have the hotel address and telephone number readily available.

Do not get into a car or accept a ride from anyone who approaches you in the airport. They may be charming, nice, speak English and polite, DO NOT go with them! This can be extremely dangerous.

Have a general idea of the hotel or train station location and how long it will take to get there. Always look at a physical or online map prior to traveling to get a general overview of the area and take note of major intersections and cross streets to use as a reference during your stay.

Climate & Packing

Climate can play a major role in your travel planning. Be sure to check the seasonal highs and lows during your trip. This will allow you to pack accordingly. Dressing in layers can be the easiest way to travel as you can take layers off when you get warm and add layers when you're cold. Pack an umbrella, the miniature size is perfect as they can be expensive when traveling and they fit perfectly in a carry-on bag.

Group Tours

I recommend investing in small group guided tours as they can take the hassle out of any trip; like eliminating lines and making the most of your time. My clients love *Paris by Paige* for the ease, in depth knowledge from someone who has lived there and peace of mind that they will have an amazing experience on my tours.

There should be free time incorporated into every tour so you have time to relax and enjoy the experience. I always infuse a bit of fun in my tours by listening to my clients and customizing the tour for their best travel experience.

CHAPTER TWO

✍

Safe Travel for Women

For most of my professional career I traveled alone or with a work colleague. I did not have the luxury of taking my family along in the early years. I will never miss those nights of arriving in a new destination late at night, not having the foresight to get food ahead of time and staying in my hotel room until the next morning because the neighborhood was not favorable. These are the situations that you have to prepare for when traveling.

My most practical tip for travel is a door stop. This $5.00 wedge from the local hardware store can save your life. It did for me.

It was my third time visiting Bangkok, Thailand, so I was comfortable with the city. I had chosen a new hotel in a new neighborhood so I could discover more of the city. I found my hotel with ease and headed to my room. It was lovely and had a balcony with a view of the Chao Phraya River.

As I unpacked my suitcase and turned on the TV, I thought what an awesome stay this was going to be. I was wrong. I always carry several door stops with me when I travel, so I put my trusty door stop in the door and proceeded to take a shower. I dressed in comfy clothes to relax for the evening. Then it happened. A man tried to enter my hotel room. With all his might, he tried to push down the door. My door stop held and I was able to call the front desk for help. Had I not had it along and stuck under the door, I am not sure what might have happened.

Hotel awareness & Check-in Tips

Try to do hotel and location research prior to arrival. Always know where you will be staying the first evening. There should be no guessing or surprises with this.

Paige's Tips:

*Pick a hotel in a safe neighborhood and/or near your meeting place.

*Pick a hotel based on the activities that you will be doing during your trip (like in a central location).

*Print out your reservation confirmation, especially if you booked it online.

*Call and confirm your booking directly with the hotel.

*Know the check-in and check-out times, and ask if there is a locked luggage room available.

*Be sure to check for the nearest exits and know the fire safety procedures. This information is usually located behind the door. Be familiar with the location of the stairs and the difference between the ground and the first floor as that may vary depending on which country you are visiting.

*Never let anyone unverified into your room. If someone claims that they are from maintenance or room service, call the front desk to verify.

*Use only your initials when making reservations and on your travel credit card. There should be no indication whether you are a female or male.

*Use a laminated business card on your luggage so your home address is not revealed in case your luggage is lost or stolen.

Hotel Room Requests

Request a room on the club floor and/or quiet floor of a hotel. Club floors have limited access from general hotel guests and require an elevator key or special elevator for entry. They usually have extra amenities like a common room, hors d'oeuvres and cocktails, and turn down service. This area of the hotel may have additional costs, but the extra layer of security is worth it in my opinion. Also, there is usually a butler or an attendant for the guests that can alert the general manager if you are missing for a while.

Choose a room away from the elevator/ice machine for reduced traffic. This keeps you one step safer from random individuals approaching your room. You may have to be adamant about this request, but it is quite important if you are a women traveling alone.

Carry a small flashlight in your briefcase or bag. I use mine frequently as each hotel room has a different setup and I have hit my knee on the nightstand on more than one occasion. Also, a flashlight beam may stun an attacker long enough to allow you to run away and get help.

Never Reveal Information

Never reveal your hotel information, especially your room number. Have the hotel clerk write it down. If the clerk says your room number out loud, ask to speak to a manager and request another room. Your safety matters.

I have a frightening, yet true story to share with you. I was standing in line at the front desk of a 4 star hotel in the United States. A man in his mid 30s, wearing a white button down shirt and khaki trousers stood to my right.

I assumed he was waiting to check out and was being courteous by letting me check in first. However, I was wrong. This man was stalking the front desk, just waiting to see if he could get information about women checking in to the hotel.

Later that evening I overheard the hotel staff talking about a situation that had occurred right after check-in. This man found out the room number of a female hotel guest by lingering around the front desk and tried to break into her hotel room to assault her. He did not realize that the time he used to get ready for the crime was just enough time for her husband, who had been parking the car, to make it to the room and enter. The man knocked on her door and told her that she had dropped something at the front desk and he wanted to be sure to get it back to her. As she cracked the door, he barged in to attack her. The husband was in the restroom and heard everything. He came out, tackled the guy and held him while his wife called the front desk and 911.

There have been times when I have put not only my door stop, but a chair behind my hotel room door. There are some cities I feel safe in and others where I do not. Learn to trust your gut and it will never lead you astray.

Paige's Tips:

*Always meet co-workers in the lobby and/or breakfast room of the hotel.

*Choose hotels with interior/corridor rooms. Avoid outside, drive up rooms if possible. I will pay extra for a non-motel type room.

*Know the local emergency contact telephone numbers for police and fire teams. Each area may have a different telephone exchange so verify ahead of time.
In Paris, I like to know the location of the nearest fire/police department. If I need to get there quickly, I will recognize either the sign or street.

*Write the emergency services information on a little card, it is especially handy if you do not speak the language.

Concierge

The concierge team could be your best friend in a new destination, as they are the ultimate insiders. They can get you a reservation for hard to get restaurants, that hot ticket you have been wanting for a venue, and provide great recommendations. They are the eyes and ears of every bustling city. Be friendly and you'll get the best service. Most four and five Star hotels will have a full-time concierge staff available for its guests.

Have a Backup Plan

The day for your Parisian vacation is here. Your passport is in hand and your bags are packed. All of your reservations are made and you are ready to go. The ride to the airport is quick and you breeze through airport security. You grab a large bottle of water and Greek Chicken salad for the flight and you wait patiently until

Section A is called for initial boarding. Pre-boarding has begun as you do one final electronics check to be sure all of your devices are fully charged. Then it is show time, "Section A".

You line up, secure your seat and the coveted overhead space, and get settled in for a quick 7 hour non-stop flight to Charles de Gaulle. You have done this routine 20 times before so you know the drill. It takes another 35 minutes before all of the passengers are on board and the flight attendants are doing their demo and pre-flight safety checks. The captain announces that we are ready for take-off. Here we go! About 1 hour into the flight you bring out your InStyle magazine and finally get relaxed in your seat when the captain announces, "Ladies and Gentlemen, this is the Captain speaking, I regret to inform you that we have seen smoke in the cockpit and are returning back to New York City immediately, please remain calm and we will keep you posted."

Did he just say what you think he said? Yes he did. The plane safely lands back in NYC and everyone is asked to remain onboard for further instructions. You find out that the arrival time in Paris will be delayed by 6 hours. But wait, you have a car waiting for you, and how do you contact the hotel? What on earth do you do next?

You may have all of your plans laid out but what do you do when there is a hiccup? It happens to the best of us, the flight is delayed and/or cancelled; the hotel is not quite what you expected; the neighborhood is scary and your host is a bit wacky. This inevitably happens to travelers every day. Having a backup plan is important to ease your mind. Indeed, make sure you have the funds, name, address and contact phone number of hotels, alternative sleeping arrangements and contacts each time you travel. You never know when you might need it.

Technology

Technology is a wonderful thing. It helps us keep in touch with family and loved ones. However, don't post your whereabouts on Social Media channels like Facebook and Twitter.

Checking in at a location and/or restaurant is not suggested as there may be predators lurking online and in the parking lot. This has opened people up for thefts, robberies and worse.

A couple who traveled to Las Vegas put their itinerary online, and while they were gone, their house was robbed. And that is not the worst part, they won $2000 at the casino and took selfies announcing their winnings. Criminals looked up #TreasureIsland, and saw all their information, including a smiling photo. They were held up at gunpoint.
Do not give away any specific information, ever.

The best way to travel is to not make yourself a target for predators. Be aware of your surroundings, and have your wits about you.

Telephone

Telephone use while traveling can be expensive, confusing and overwhelming. Telephone calls can start at $5.99 USD per minute and data charges start at $20.00 USD and go upwards from there for most US carriers. I advise people to not use their existing data on their phone and to turn that feature off. Use local and hotel wi-fi when available. Each telecommunications carrier has its own pricing plan and roaming charges, ask ahead of time for a breakdown of these charges. You can always sign up for an international calling plan or use a removable sim card for your phone. You can also purchase a telephone once you get to the destination if you plan on an extended stay. There are international calling and prepaid cards available for purchase as well. Calling from your hotel room can be an expensive option. I never use this option. You can use Skype and Facetime to connect with family and friends if available.

CHAPTER THREE

Women Traveling Alone

Safety is your primary concern when traveling alone and it is appropriate to ask your destination contact or corporate colleague about it. A woman traveling alone must be prepared for any situation.

I have been extremely lucky during my years of traveling solo, however luck can run out if you are not careful and aware of your surroundings. If you are traveling solo and happen to be walking alone or -in the evening-casually join a group of people near you.

Here is something that happened to me a couple of years ago.

It was a warm, Indian summer Sunday, and I decided to take a walk to discover a new neighborhood in Paris. I was walking alone when I noticed out of the corner of my eye a man in a dark blue, two-door car trying to get my attention. I quickly looked away and tried to ignore him, but it was apparent that he had been watching me for a while. When I slowed down, he slowed down, when I sped up, he sped up. I knew where the police station was and adjusted my route to get me there. I got that uneasy feeling that makes the hair on the back of your neck stand up. I continued along the rue Guy Lussac and SO DID HE! There happened to be a family walking slightly ahead of me and when they all stopped to look at a historical sign, I stopped with them, like I was a part of their group. The man finally drove away. If you are ever in a similar situation, think ahead and use your wits. I am convinced this saved my life.

Be Aware of your Surroundings

It is important to be aware of your surroundings. You must pay attention to local laws, customs and neighborhoods. Do not travel alone at night or linger in isolated areas. Be familiar with local areas and always ask questions regarding safety for women.

Unwanted Advances

You may have to handle unwanted advances or attention during your travels. If this happens try to find the nearest police officer or security guard. If possible remove yourself from the situation quickly. Be direct and strong with your words. Walk with confidence and with your head held high. Do not worry about seeming rude. Being unfriendly can be the sign needed to have others leave you alone. Act as if you know where you are going and not like the typical tourist. Before leaving your hotel have a route planned and look for land markers to make your journey easier. Unfortunately the US and other developed nations do not release reliable data on the number of women assaulted annually and that is very frightening. If you or someone you know do happen to be a victim of sexual assault, notify the authorities immediately or as soon as you can. There may be valuable evidence that can be gathered and used for prosecution. Contact the Office of Overseas Citizens Services or the U.S. Embassy or Consulate nearest to you.

I am married now, but when I was single and traveling, all during my 20s and 30s, I wore a huge costume jewelry ring and told men that my NFL player husband was waiting for me back at the hotel or nearest café. It worked every time.

Role of Women

Be sure to do some online research of women's roles in your destination location. This is very important and should not be skipped. Some cultures do not extend the same working conditions and professional courtesies to Western women. They may even interpret our demeanor as aggressive and promiscuous. Knowing that in Saudi Arabia and India, people of the opposite sex should not touch for any reason, including shaking hands is very important to the cross cultural experience and your safety.

Machismo

This is meant to be an assessment, not a slight. Asian/Middle Eastern/Latin America cultures may exhibit machismo within their communities. This basically means that men are taken far more seriously than women and their manners and interactions with women may reflect this antiquated attitude. You will be treated differently because you are a woman. It is not your imagination. Be acutely aware of men while you are traveling: the man staring from the doorway, the group of young men hanging on the corner, and the young professional looking at you on the Metro. Women are treated this way whether they are local or a foreigner. Stay confident, move quickly and remove yourself from any dangerous environments as fast as you can. Being aware of this cultural difference can save your life no matter what continent that you are on.

Escorts

This is not the kind that you may be thinking of, however it may be required that you have a male escort in some countries, either to be out in the community or even to drive. In Saudi Arabia you will need a male escort as it is the law, and for your own protection. Your travel agent, guide, or host, may be able to help you make arrangements for these types of services while visiting.

It may cost little more, but I would suggest hiring a guide, driver, and or interpreter if you are going to an unknown region or country. Remember, your safety is paramount.

Self-Defense

The tenets of self-defense include being aware of your surroundings, taking action when needed and having the right attitude. It is the best method of defending yourself against attackers and one more way to be self-reliant. I have taken self-defense classes and encourage other women to learn several women's safety techniques. A self-defense class is always a recommendation, as it can provide you with a few practical tactics to ward off an attacker. You can find classes in your local community or through recreation departments.

Drinking & Partying

I am all for having a good time, however, you have to be extra careful no matter how old or young you are. Going to clubs and bars are a part of the traveler's experience, but women need to be extra careful. If you do drink while traveling, be especially vigilant about the new influx of date rape drugs on the scene. One such drug is Rohypnol, an odorless, colorless and tasteless drug that has made many unsuspecting women victims of predators. The effects can be displayed in as short as ten minutes and last up to hours. Some victims have been known to blackout for up to twenty four hours and have respiratory distress. Always keep your glass with you at all times, buy or pour your own drink if the opportunity presents itself. Keep an eye on the bartender as well as he could be in cooperation with the perpetrators. As an added note, the alcohol content may be higher than what you are used to in the US or Canada. Some beers and ciders can be strong and may affect you differently.

Smoking

If you smoke, know the local rules and regulations for smoking. Over 110 countries worldwide have banned smoking in public places. Restaurants and bars may be restricted and there may be hefty fines if you are found in violation. In 2007, France enforced strict smoking laws. It is now illegal to smoke in offices, government buildings, schools and restaurants. Cigarettes can be expensive outside of the US as well.

Clothing

Conservative dress is recommended. I usually take my cue from local women and do as much research as I can to dress like a local. There are many resources online. When entering churches or places of worship it is advisable to have your shoulders and knees covered. Shy away from shorts or anything too revealing. I travel with dresses and long skirts. Women in most foreign countries tend to clothe themselves a little dressier than Americans. Keep that in mind as you make your wardrobe choices. Leave all expensive jewelry at home as you would be heartbroken if your great-grandmother's ring was lost or stolen.

Pack light. If you are burdened with several pieces of luggage it puts you in prime position as a victim and your reaction time is decreased.

Loneliness & Homesickness

Sometimes loneliness sets in but it is usually temporary. Being away from family and friends can be challenging, whether you are working, volunteering or vacationing while traveling. Homesickness can affect people in different ways. You are in unfamiliar territory, you are away from your normal routines, food can be strange, and local culture totally foreign. Calling home and being in contact online is a great way to cure this.

As a tourist you can integrate into the local community by hanging out where the locals do and attending local events. When I lived in France, I loved hosting family and friends who were visiting Paris. It provided me with a much needed connection to the familiar and sharing my love for another culture with them. This really helped set the stage for my boutique travel company, **Paris by Paige** (http://www.parisbypaige.com) where I guide small and private groups around Paris. I would strongly suggest creating a new routine for yourself and stay as healthy as possible.

LGBT

If you are a Lesbian, Gay, Bisexual, or Transgender traveler, ask for recommendations prior to travel for hotels, clubs, restaurants, and bars from family and friends. There are also websites that cater to destination specific questions. More hotel brands like Hilton and Marriot have created special vacation booking sites specifically for the lesbian and gay market. See the resource list at the end of the book for suggestions. When you travel you will find that there are friendly neighborhoods in each city, which make a better travel experience. Research online and ask friends. In Paris, there is a bustling scene in the Marais and it has at least four newspapers with local events, meetings and is a wonderful place for a honeymoon.

Traveling alone has opened many doors for me both professionally and personally. I learned how to be alone with myself and my thoughts. I learned how to interact with others through my own initiation. I learned to be extra aware of my surroundings and learned to be street savvy. I learned to read maps, new languages and how to lower my voice an entire octave when answering the phone. I learned how to entertain myself and not need to have another person present during my adventures.

Your time is your own and your independence and self-confidence is bound to soar to new heights. Try traveling alone sometime, you may surprise and delight yourself.

CHAPTER FOUR

Business Travel

Business Travel

When traveling for business, it is important to prepare not only for the travel but also to expect tangible results from the business trips. Companies invest millions of dollars annually in business travel and want to keep their Executives and Associates safe during travel. My most important tip for business travel is to have a contact in your destination to help mitigate any unforeseen challenges.

An example of the importance of having a contact in the visiting country comes from my corporate career. There were clients that purchased our tour product through their travel agent for a 21 day Yangtze River cruise in China. There flights were as follows: New York-Tokyo-Beijing. Upon leaving the United States and heading to Japan, the ticket agent checked their passport validity and asked them if they had their "Visa." They responded, "yes," and proceeded on their flight to Tokyo. As they were connecting, the Japanese agent looked over their passports and found that there was no "Entry Visa for China" and denied boarding. The two passengers insisted that they had a "Visa." This conversation went on for about 20 minutes and it was nearing the time for departure. The Japanese agent then said, "If you have a Visa, then show it to me." And you can guess, the American passenger pulled out his wallet to show his "Visa" credit card. This was not the correct "Visa." By the time they called us, they had tried to contact their travel agent to no avail, who had not informed them of this critical requirement. They had missed their connecting flight and had only 2 days to get to the cruise ship before departure. I was able to use my contacts and connections in both China and Japan to get a representative to escort the couple to the Chinese Embassy and get an "emergency visa" to continue on their trip. If I had not established those relationships, they would have lost $15,000 and the experience of a lifetime.

Foreign Languages

We've all heard it before: Communication is key, but how exactly does that apply to travel? Communication is a combination of both verbal and non-verbal cues.

Foreign languages are critical to business success when working on an international team. Executives should try to learn basic greetings in the destination language. You can take a language class or get a tutor prior to departure. There are several online language programs like Rosetta Stone and Pimsleur that are excellent for learning. Be able to use common phrases like hello, good bye, thank you, and please. I advise my executive and professional clients to attempt to have an assigned contact in the destination. This can be an essential asset to the enjoyment of your working experience.

Connections

It is good to have a connection pathway back to your home and/or business. Using e-mail, text, social media and skype really simplifies the process. Most hotels and restaurants have wi-fi/internet for free or minimal cost. Be sure to ask the staff for the necessary passwords and access. Most major US hotel chains also have a business center for their guests. Check the website for details and pricing.

Free wi-fi is usually available either in your room, common areas or the hotel lobby. Protect yourself and your device with hotspot access by turning on your firewall and limiting file sharing.

Travel Documentation

Be diligent with all travel documentation. Have copies of e-tickets/itineraries/rental car information with you at all times. If you are renting a car, arrange for someone to escort you in parking lots, especially if you are arriving late at night or early in the morning.

Have a list of supplier telephone numbers, just in case. You can either print this out and have it in your purse, or e-mail it directly to your smartphone and/or tablet. Include your internal travel coordinator if it is applicable.

I always like to have contact names and numbers in case of an emergency. By having it in one place makes it easier to locate and use.

Travel Apps

Use travel apps for compiling all of your itinerary information and reservations.

I use an app for all of my itineraries like TripIt and Worldmate; you can put all of your information into one location for easy retrieval.

Paige's favorites:

*Trip Advisor Offline City Guides, I love the up-to-date city maps that they offer.

*Hipmunk-flight and hotel app is color coded and informational.

*Kayak-air and hotel search app.

*Hotel Tonight-last minute available destination specific hotel rooms.

*Your favorite major airline online app (American, United, Air France, etc.)

Paige's Tips:

*Know the address and location of your nearest English-speaking embassy, either USA, Canada, Great Britain or Australia. These embassies may be able to assist you if the US Embassy is not available. Write down each of their addresses on a note card and carry it with you.

*Always check to be sure there are no travel advisories issued by the US State Department. Their website provides the most current and up to date information.

*Carry multiple photocopies of your passport in separate locations.

*Have a home contact with a copy of your passport for emergencies. They will be able to get it to you right away if you need it.

CHAPTER FIVE

✍

International Cultural Taboos

Traveling internationally for business can be both rewarding and challenging. Research hierarchy and protocol for all of your business interactions. This can make or break your deal. I have seen deals falter due to poor manners and etiquette. It is vital to know proper etiquette in all business and personal situations.

Proper forms of greetings

Knowing the proper form of greeting is crucial when traveling. Whether you are embarking on a new country or even a new corporate culture, this can make or break a deal for you. It is extremely important to know that the interaction between men and women varies from country to country. For instance, the Chinese always use titles when addressing someone verbally. And there may be situations where as a woman, despite your C-suite position, the CEO of an Asian company may not speak to you directly. He may instruct his assistant to do so. Do not be offended. Do your research ahead of time and you will be prepared for the situation. In some Middle Eastern countries it is not permissible for men and women to touch under any circumstances, including shaking hands. Office buildings and universities may have separate entrances for men and women. Historically, if unlawful mixing is discovered, criminal charges may be filed and usually women face harsher punishments.

Hierarchy is extremely important and should always be considered. This can range from job title, family structure, to age. Asking personal questions upon meeting someone for the first time is also looked down upon.

Hand gestures can play a major role in this as well. In America the "A-OK" sign is favorable, however, in other countries it is seen as the "evil eye" and it can be interpreted that you are casting the evil eye on them. So always use your hands with caution.

Business cards -Dual Language & Etiquette

Be aware of the cultural nuances of your destination and their business practices. Find out if a dual language or translated card is necessary as Asian and Middle Eastern countries do prefer them. Most countries prefer cards to be presented with your right hand only, as presenting any other way can be considered offensive. Standard Protocol and presenting etiquette indicates that you start with the most Senior Executive after the formal introduction is made. For example, in Japan present with two hands, with Japanese side facing up. In China, never write on a business card.

Know the meaning of eye contact in your destination country. In Argentina, Canada and North America, looking someone directly in the eyes conveys trustworthiness. In Asian countries however this would be considered aggressive or pushy. In some parts of Southern Europe and the Middle East, it is seen as a sexual invitation. Be careful with voice and volume control when having face-to-face communications in France, as they dislike loud and boisterous talking. Check it out the next time you are in a crowded restaurant. You will observe most people leaning in to have conversations on a more intimate level. This is a subtle, yet powerful cultural difference.

CHAPTER SIX

✍

Clothing

Clothing

A capsule wardrobe philosophy for travel is the best way to go. It makes dressing easier and your suitcase lighter. A capsule wardrobe uses one color scheme to mix and the inclusion of accessories. I recommend that you plan to be dressier than in the US if traveling internationally. From my extensive travel experience I have noticed that women in most major cities dress fashionably. Dressing in layers also makes it easier to adapt to any temperature or climate.

Paige's clothing list for a week-long trip:

*2 slacks/pants
*1 jeans (dark colored)

*light weight jacket/blazer/sweater
*2 dresses (short or maxi)
*2 tops
*2 tanks/t-shirts
*scarf
*pajamas
*mini umbrella
*sunglasses
*comfortable shoes/booties/ballet flats
*cross body handbag
*toiletries
*makeup

Conservative or local dress is recommended when traveling. Not only is it important to dress professionally, one should also be comfortable. My non-negotiable for travel: comfortable shoes, including heels. The last thing you need is to be in a situation where you cannot walk, let alone run for your life.

Never wear new shoes while traveling, no matter how cute they are. Break them in for at least a month before an international trip.

I must admit that I am a dress addict and I will rock one anywhere. They are versatile and fun, they can be sassy, sophisticated, short, or long. You can generally find one in your favorite color and they provide comfort when appropriate. I always pack dresses as the staples of my travel wardrobe. One day I may even start a travel dress clothing line, you heard it here first.

CHAPTER SEVEN

∾

Packing Light

Pack Light

Packing light is my number one tip for any traveling woman for business or pleasure. We tend to over pack and then we pay the consequences with back pain and hefty airline baggage fees. I am definitely not the travel hack that can get a month's worth of clothing into a backpack, but I do have a few packing tricks to share with you.

Always pack based on the capsule wardrobe method and mix and match from a neutral palette. It makes combining pieces easier and a snap to coordinate. Choose clothing that are wrinkle resistant and professional. Remember to dress in layers for varying temperature changes as it is one of the best ways to handle these fluctuations. I love traveling with a pashmina shawl or scarf that can be used for drafty airplanes and restaurants; plus they are fashionable. I do have a video on how to tie a simple and elegant scarf.

Invest in a quality suitcase that is easy to maneuver and carry. I like suitcases on wheels or with a roller board and 4 wheels are better than 2. It makes for quick retrieval as well as navigating airports easier.

Every female traveler must **LOVE** her carry-on bag as it will be with you at all times. You really want one that is cute, functional and a reflection of your personality. This sassy bag is the travel-home for your personal items, electronics and medications. I include my wallet and a tech pack (a small bag for all of my chargers and cords).
I do not carry a large purse when I travel, I keep it to a minimum, pack my purse in my luggage and carry a clutch that can fit into my cute carry-on bag. It is one less thing to be accountable for during travel.

For more resources about packing light be sure to check out the suggested websites in the resource section.

Pack a few days ahead of time to do clothing repairs or make adjustments. Then take out half of what you have packed and **PACK LIGHT!**

CHAPTER EIGHT

Finances

Finances

Being a victim of financial theft while traveling is not only devastating during your trip but also a mess to clean up when you get home. It is critical that you do everything you can to prevent being a victim. Exchange about $100 in local currency before you travel and have a backup bank card with funds available in the case of an emergency. I recommend a prepaid and supported travel card like American Express or AAA.

Alert your banking institution of your travel itinerary and the countries that you will be visiting. It is also advisable to know what your daily spending limits are to avoid potential embarrassment. Guess who has experienced that? You got it. Me. It was a hot August day and I had just arrived in Hong Kong. It was my first trip there and I was very excited. We flew through customs and headed to our harbor front hotel. As we were checking into our hotel there was a problem with my credit card. It was denied and locked. I didn't know what to think, I had no idea what was going on. This was the first time anything like this had ever happened to me. All that I knew was that my credit card did not work and it was my main source of funding for this business trip. I made a call to my bank in the US to resolve the situation and that long distance call to my local bankS from Kowloon was not cheap. My card was denied because I did not inform them that I would be traveling in Hong Kong, let alone in Asia. I learned my lesson and was happy that my bank was looking out for me.

Being aware of the different types of credit cards worldwide can be crucial. Chip credit cards are the norm in Europe and most American cards are not yet equipped with this microchip. I have seen the aftermath of this in the metro station at Versailles. It is not a pretty picture as people line up to get tickets and are unable to purchase them because their cards are not working. If a manual cashier is not available you are out of luck. Have a transportation card or carry local cash for such instances.

ATM for withdrawing money

Using the ATM while traveling is easy to do and quite accessible. It is a great way to secure cash and exchange money in local currencies. I recommend that you use Travel, Business or Prepaid credit cards to minimize damage if your card gets stolen as it will not be connected to your personal account at home. These cards offer additional services and protection if they are lost or stolen. I have found that I get the best exchange rates by using my card. Perform your ATM transactions during the day and be aware of your surroundings. Be aware of credit card scanners on ATMs as well, which may lead to identity theft issues. Just look over the ATM prior to using for anything that looks unusual. Most European ATMs require a four (4) digit pin number to operate. If your pin does not fit this specification, contact your financial institution to make an adjustment prior to travel.

In the case of an emergency, it is important to have a way for someone to send you money from home (wire money/MoneyGram transfer/Western Union/American Express/Thomas Cook). Wire transfers are cheaper but some banks only give you the funds in local currency, so be sure to ask ahead of time. Always ask about the current exchange rate as well because you do not want to lose out on the conversion. Be patient as wire transfers may take a few days to complete. Western Union is faster but it can be expensive so be sure to weigh all of your options.

Tipping

Be aware of tipping practices while you travel. In some countries, like France, the service fee is included in the price in bars and restaurants. If the service is incredible, I will round the bill up. Just do some research ahead of time.

Theft prevention

Passports, credit cards and extra money should be secured in a chest or waist money belt. A good practice would be to only have your daily expenses in your purse and put the rest in a secure location. Pocket scarves and camisoles are perfect for hiding valuables.

When traveling in first, second, and third world countries, I carry all of my valuables in my money belt. I refuse to be a victim, and do what I can to prevent any incidents.

Right out of college, my colleagues and I decided to do a girls' long weekend trip in Europe. We were three young ladies traveling in the middle of France and having a blast. Until . . . the hotel staff robbed us of our paper airplane tickets (you remember those, right?) and cash; our valuables were in the room safe. I ended up having a heated argument with the hotel proprietor in French. We went to the police station to file a report but they did not help us. From that day forward, I never leave anything of value in my room.

Try to travel with a minimum of electronics (phone, ipad, laptop). You do not want to be overloaded and responsible for too many items while traveling.

Paige's Tips:
*Use the hotel's large safe instead of the smaller room safe to secure your valuables.

*Keep all valuables on your person if it is safe to do so.

*Limit the number of valuables that you travel with; less is better.

CHAPTER NINE

❧

Staying Healthy

Staying Healthy

Starting out your travel adventure healthy is the best way to go. Try to be in your best shape prior to departure.

Healthcare systems vary throughout the world and can be excellent, poor, or disorganized. Doctor services may be a fraction of the cost they are in the United States. There may be a hotel physician on site or on call for guest use. The US Embassy usually has a list of English-speaking physicians if necessary.

Make sure your childhood vaccinations are up to date and inquire if you need additional ones based on your travel destinations. Plan enough time for the entire course of treatment as it could take several months to be effective. You can consult the Centers for Disease Control (CDC) for recommended immunizations.

Pharmacies may be the best place to initially get medical attention. Many pharmacists may be medically trained and could be open late at night. I have found that they usually speak English and can help with most issues. Look for specific colored signs and symbols to indicate a pharmacy. In France the pharmacy is indicated by a bright green cross. In the US, a red cross indicates first aid assistance.

And don't forget to get a dental checkup and have dental procedures completed prior to departure. Being in severe tooth pain will affect your travel experience.

Medical Treatment

If you do have a serious illness or infection that requires medical treatment, ask where the locals go. There may or may not be an English-speaking hospital, so you want the next best thing. Medical care in emerging and other countries may be a fraction of the price for treatment in the United States. Get the help you need and get it right away. I suggest getting the assistance of a translator to help with medical terminology and prescription instructions. You may not have a clear head from the illness and two heads are better than one in critical times. Also notify the US Embassy if you have to hospitalized for an extended period as they can keep your family abreast of your situation if need be.

Medication and Medical Devices

Always put your medications (original containers) in your carry-on bag and not in your checked luggage, as it may be lost or stolen. If you have severe allergies, be sure to carry an EpiPen and a copy of the doctor's prescription. If your medication requires refrigeration, please make arrangements prior to travel with the airlines and hotels.

Have a prescription and generic medication list as name brands vary from country to country. Write it on a card and carry it with you. A signed prescription by a doctor may be required for narcotics and/or syringe-administered medications. This could affect diabetic supplies and other medications.

Paige's Tips:
*Pack a small first-aid kit to include the following:
-Tylenol (aches and pain)
-Aspirin
-chewable Pepto-Bismol (diarrhea)
-band-aids (cuts and burns)
-Neosporin (antibiotic ointment)
- Hydrocortisone cream 1%
-Desitin
-Benadryl (allergies)
-sunscreen
-moleskin (blisters)
-eye drops (dry eyes & polluted air)
-tweezers (splinters)
-small scissors
-small sewing kit (repairs)
-hand sanitizer
-soap

Take a thermometer along. It is easy to pack and a quick indicator if you are not feeling well. And don't forget to wear sunscreen to protect your skin at all times.
Sightseeing and relaxing at the beach can be painful if you are not careful.

Drugs and Alcohol

Have you seen the TV show *Locked Up Abroad*? It is worth noting that laws vary drastically on the use of drugs and alcohol and some countries have hefty fines and jail time. Did you know that it is only legal for a Rastafarian to smoke marijuana in Jamaica? Everyone else is subject to prosecution. Alcohol and coffee can make you dehydrated so be aware of the local laws regarding consumption. Travel insurance claims can be deemed invalid if drinking is involved.

Stay Hydrated

Staying hydrated is important when traveling by airplane, car, and train.
Use bottled and purified water in destinations with questionable water sources, including when brushing your teeth. Stick to food that has been cooked and/or has a peel. Stay away from ice as it is made with the local water supply. You do not want to fall victim to any intestinal ailments. My husband found that out the hard way during a vacation in Costa Rica. He thought it would be refreshing to enjoy a shaved ice from a street vendor. Boy was he wrong.

Health & Travel Insurance

Be sure to check your insurance policy for all its stipulations. Check with your general insurance coverage for international and out of network coverage as there may be exclusions that you are not aware of.

Your current health insurance coverage may offer special inclusions while traveling, so call and check before buying additional insurance. Be sure to take a copy of your health insurance card and all telephone numbers. It may be necessary to have supplemental International and Medical Evacuation insurance. Medicare and Medicaid may not reimburse you for expenses incurred abroad.

You never know what may happen and you want to be prepared. Most major credit card companies also have some coverage for cardholders; check with them directly. You can also buy international health coverage if you plan to be traveling for an extended period of time. Please see the resource section for suggestions.

Fitness

Carry a small bottle of water with you throughout the day to stay hydrated, especially if you plan to do a lot of walking/hiking. It is always a good idea to start a mild to moderate fitness routine once your airline tickets are booked. This way you can continually build up your exercise tolerance and prepare your body and mind for the trip ahead. Some destinations are easy to navigate, while others may not have elevators or escalators. You may have to walk up 7 flights of stairs while carrying your luggage, or if the London Tube elevator breaks down at Covent Gardens, you may have to climb 150 tiny steps up a centuries old winding metal staircase just to get to street level.

Disabled Travelers

There may be limitations in the older cities for some disabled travelers. There are worldwide organizations online to answer questions and provide suggestions. Accommodations are being made slowly to address physical, hearing and visual disabilities. Stick to major hotel chains, museums and taxi transportation and if you need specific accommodations, contact the hotel to inquire what they may provide during your stay.

Personal Products

Always carry your own feminine products with you and take extra as they may be hard to find in some countries, or at premium prices. I like what I like, so I am sure to bring it along with me. Plus, I just learned from Bear Grylls that you can use a tampon to start a fire in a pinch in the wilderness. Now there is always at least one in my bag.

Safe sex is a non-negotiable; and having your own protection and condoms is necessary as they may not be available. You really never want to be caught off guard or in a sticky situation.

Toilet Envy

WC/Salerni/Toilet/Banyo/Toilette/Choo
There may be times when you encounter something from outer space behind the door that says "Bathroom." This is when the almighty 'hovering squat' comes into play. I suggest that you practice this technique to build up extra muscles 4 weeks prior to your trip. Also, bring along your personal toilet tissue in a purse-size as some bathrooms may be lacking in the toilet paper department. Some toilets are also self-cleaning, so handle your business and be quick. Some bathrooms are simply a hole in the ground, have no doors, and you may have to pay for entrance. Just embrace the experience; it will make for fun stories and travel memories. Ladies, you have been warned!

CHAPTER TEN

❧

Travel Tips

I would like to give you some of my general travel tips whether you are traveling alone or with others.

*Ask for help if needed, there is no shame in asking for assistance.

*Make sure that you have transportation arrangements for your arrival as you may be tired or disoriented.

*Use public transportation including taxis if you can. Research the public system in guide books and online prior to going.

*If you plan to rent a car, know if you there are special licenses and/or permits needed by Americans.

*Plan to learn local road signs and traffic signals of the visiting country.

*Carry an extra tote bag to bring home souvenirs and gifts. You can ship items home via the mail, which will reduce your luggage costs. The airlines now charge fees for extra luggage and these fees can be quite expensive.

*Carry a small flashlight, you can use it if the power goes out unexpectedly.

*Have an emergency cash stash on you in a hidden location or keep it in the hotel safe.

* Go with your intuition and do what is best for you.

Electrical

Electricity is different on every continent, it could be 120 or 220 volts. Not only do the currencies vary, the size of the outlets do as well. When it comes to electricity and voltage converters there are many products on the market at reasonable prices. Do your research to make sure your electronics will not be in danger.

Traveling with Children

Set boundaries and rules for children, like staying together and not touching items in stores and restaurants. Explain and reiterate "Stranger Danger" and be advised of all their activities. Let them know the dangers that exist without inducing extreme fear.

Know what costs are associated with children as they may be free and/or reduced. They may stay free at hotels, yet have to pay full price on the airplane. We love traveling with our young son and it is so refreshing to see the world through his eyes.

If you are traveling with small children be sure to have an ample supply of disposable diapers and outlet covers as these may be difficult to find depending on your travel destination.

Have and coordinate plenty of activities for all the age ranges of the children in your party. This will make the trip so much more enjoyable. We like to include our son in the planning, by bringing out a huge map prior to travel. This gives an overview of the destination, is a lesson in Geography and he feels like he is part of the trip planning.

Traveling with Pets

If you are traveling with pets make sure to adhere to airline rules and make their comfort paramount. Bring along a copy of all vaccinations and shots, you should be able to get this from your veterinarian. There are many hotels that allow your pet to stay with you. Do your research ahead of time.

Travel Wisdom

Traveling can be an incredible adventure, while creating memories of a lifetime. Personal security should always be at the forefront of your mind when traveling locally or internationally. These tips can be applied in everyday life and any situation. I love traveling and making friends along the way from all over the world. It doesn't matter what your age or background, travel brings people together. With the right planning, resources and sense of adventure, any woman can travel safely and have a great time doing it. So grab your passport, suitcase, carry-on bag and Safe Travels!

Merci for your time and attention to my safe travel strategies for women. I would love to know if this book helps you in any way or if you have your own safe travel tips. Feel free to share them with us. If you want more travel insights and bonuses, feel free to sign up for our newsletter at http://www.parisbypaige.com/books

Resources

Finances
American Express
AAA-Travel Card

Travel Apps
Trip Advisor Offline City Guides
Hipmunk
Kayak
Hotel Tonight
Trip Advisor
Hipmunk

Health
Centers for Disease Control (CDC)
Office of Overseas Citizens Services at 1-888-407-4747
(from overseas: 202-501-4444) or the U.S. Embassy or
Consulate nearest you.
http://www.medeassist.com
http://www.insuremytrip.com

LGBT
Damron Travel-LGBT
http://www.damron.com

Packing List
http://www.travelfashiongirl.com
http://www.herpackinglist.com

ABOUT THE AUTHOR

K. Paige Engle is an entrepreneur, international speaker, traveler and foreign language evangelist. She has traveled to more than 20 countries and 300 cities worldwide and loves to explore different cultures. She has a working knowledge of five languages and speak French and English fluently. Having lived in Europe and Asia she has firsthand expertise of the cultural nuances that can affect both the personal and professional experiences.

Paige splits her time between Paris, France and Milwaukee, Wisconsin. She enjoys her time with her husband, Pete and her son, Robert. She loves to laugh with her Mom & Dad and of course visit all of her friends scattered across the globe. She spends her time guiding groups around Paris, speaking to corporations and associations about safe travel strategies, writing, homeschooling, traveling with her family and eating fresh Nutella crepes.

You can follow her celebrating the French lifestyle at www.parisbypaige.com.